SUB ROSA

"under the rose"
Secrecy

SUB ROSA
THE BOOK OF METAPHYSICS

FRANCESCA LISETTE

BOILER HOUSE PRESS

I

BECOMING

ECSTASY (DISPERSAL)

Some of these poems previously appeared in the anthologies *Viersome 001* (Veer), *I Love Roses When They're Past Their Best* (Test Centre), and *Out of Everywhere 2* (Reality Street). An adaptation of *Ecstasy (Dispersal)* appears in *SPELLS: 21st Century Occult Poetry* (Lingua Ignota). Poems also appeared in the following journals: *Tripwire, dusie, Cordite Poetry Review, COVEN Berlin, disappearing curtains, Intercapillary Space,* and *The Paper Nautilus.* The poem 'From Whose Wounds Beauty Springs' was published in a commemorative newspaper for Francesca Capone's MFA Thesis show *Writing-in-Threads*.

Thanks to the editors of these publications.

*This book is for everyone who opened their
homes & their hearts to me in the last eight years
— in love & gratitude*

I

WE ARE ALL JUST PERSON PEOPLE IN A FUCKED-UP UNIVERSE
for Josh

we are all just person people
in a fucked-up universe
wake up. good
morning is the same as night
unpick stealth of wool & teeth it's knotted in.
let's start again, because gender theory has been
inadequate unless lived inhabited as part of daily drum
roll that reaches forgotten angst you can't itch.
like this could be a rinse of past life, wiped out
by the sink of relentless impasse & begin again,
too cool for memories. eyes flick over a split-level
dust cloud   who have we been   where we've fucked
or not eyeballs to fluid   it caves in   because don't
straighten this acceptance   anything   not goading it
isn't, doesn't exist   outside the prism   of illusion
words   carry in a string   cauterising your ear
to my lip   just south of London   & could the
cabinet of affections play with provable value, at
what point does the refusal of bourgeois morality
become self-neglect, those who can think about
deprivation are provided for, & how percolating
these disavowed hands make the cross, scuffed w/
poverty dis(-solution/ -illusion) compression it all
acts to the same breath telescoped thru your vigil as
you rise to shave   hued vassal in morning light
have i ever cared enough burnished to distraction
& the echo of endlessness because raw, prescient
as smoke funnelling over Wordsworth's mystic
house and past lives are gone and scream because this is
true economics slide by oil-black ——— are never
coming back the opportunity to be free of prose
return to basin and strip the head's colour-swatch
to this premise we'll be rid of tomorrow   25/01

sometimes always. the virgin is

step out w/ panels stretched wingform

corrective vision untrammelled
burden stringing intransigent global cosmetic
standard, yet gospel skeleton is restive in the wind.
formless *reductio*: opacity blurred for
tonic privacy
& breathe again, waxy carrier entrusts
a pagan restorative birth ritual
discloses not emphatic fish anomie of
gentle lung; scissoring its own pain,
plural windows replicating the retreated stars.
not wholly this.
a spot holds
co-existing plates to account, shyness
fault shared. occasionally
it flickers into my consciousness that it is
 one of 7 billion, not folding its
 insignificance into a hurtless line
(the line is clear) rather gutted into maintenance,
non-insistent cupole for cascading sentience
  is a spark, despite
interrupted will surfeiting each
midnight's dance
 a final day. hands shiver in time to situated prisons
& disorder returns over the silent and black trees.

ON BEING AN ANGEL
for Francesca Woodman

1.

To use this dark & silence, out of which no solid mass can
distinguish itself, but moves with a bird's low whirr.
Colossus capita articulated damage fragments.
Moving through a looseness of trees groping headline
aghast, toll booth wrist mania
        deletes a wash of primary colour
                    erases the light off a face held in late prose
                & also masks her magnifying signature.
                        her: a stillness signified thru
                            immediate absence
ope the bank of face disclosing curiosity, jerking
a window under gentle erotics of time &
    shaping the milk-run wood's collaboration with
block of white unsheltered, melting starkness.

2.

World is it; spaced in actions, afternoon use for nails
    other than biting, tawny fabric gripped in
 all-natural conscription
                                lap folded yet escaping the 'posed'
Dirty down to the bristles fear works harder
    splices mouth to brick ignite shelter
                            laid down upon because
there was no-one you could talk to
crystal porpoise struck a note topaz: shaky calves
    on dull prism sweat and breath dope the glass
pour a subject carousel, bleed stockinged lace
incarnate flesh dissolving swift as a
child's head under water however more or less
1 pound of bone amounts to inviolate materials

testify in the slow dark: salvific humour in the masculine,
your water-broken moon, your angular absorption;
the house of sly ponies, in which hours wandered
doorless rooms slack-shadowed, a thousand suns
detached & floating like eyes;
your subtle penis, your maiden boots,
     your earthing by name.

March indescribable devolving into a factotum, a.
A private museum. Strangled cords melt the
precise flesh of friends/ pop-eye filth
gathering in a steam world, hub of
purpling ticks. You knock me sideways
crescent across the table not speaking to
disturbs the present's slow curl of disease.

Wipe back foot after coming
home lazy, in defeat
where do the skies fit
under all this we into & rubber.

Last time I lay down it was to lie next to you.
Dubbed whyte feminism punk road movie
shut out a calling card who soaps tarot speech
anatomy bundle, she says, but famish or pick
at a waiting clit.

FED ON SCARLET HIPS

My lover's thoughts are not
                        of me at all.

— John Wieners

Decorticated, time is deliquescent
echolocation.

Eternity sprung back ineluctably thru
my lover's lips

Hush
& stagger   across
  softly spoken ways.

Time-stuck
  fool's paradise
sings in the fabric of
your skin

Borne, a studded
bird-mass is loaded w/
fortune primaries,
fruit of a thousand
sorrows.

My heart is a clip
for speaking with.

LANGUAGE LANGUAGE LANGUAGE LANGIUGE LANGAUGE

Embryo spoiled
in a dark bleat of snow.
What lives in a wrinkled
condom
          Mine.

The fast losses of an hour. Your blue disturbia in the sunshine
& amitriptyline coating sags, mixing the green and the brown.
Detach speaking cord and wrap around dogs
who are not us,
leafed and debarred. Costco Amy
weeps. What is to weep. Is to Ophelia'z
drownin dress blooms. Discordance
can make you happy, can make a joke
of death. Living thinks you. The trying-
to is actually beautiful.

*

Weakness a problem for art. During fashion
artifice is set afloat on a membrane of safety
for locks' quavers. Indiscernible trouble
around the lower mandibular gums. The recesses
get caught in a tongue. One is hardly at a
pertinence to explain
gestures under office. Is a flesh a loot
undived.

*

Quarrel me hearts to set aflame in evening's
slow glare or a ribcage yanks off an ear
& is a child again, luring out frolics
for shame. Love is not a breathing thing
Smirched with sighs, until it walks out
alone. The house I lived with turns
to a clatter of nature sounds neither
done or retrieved.
Ague mental.

*

Vulnerability is specificity, or anything
plays into the question of trust
remaindered in darkness, where sickling
angels capsize & spread. Eleven eleven
: lust in foreground enmity is barrier
broke, disconnect sugaring leaves in layers.
Promise me, sailor? – that only reality strips
bare feet with hot tarmac and shit under
my fingernails, from loving you
keep only what I can't touch
winter's ecstasy behind.

*The heart's deviations, rendered as psychopathology. Now to
love and betray, to love love, to seek betrayal to return one to love,
to find love and betrayal inseparable, is there a pathology?
Or a clinical pastoral? Or?*
   — Wendy Mulford, *La Pitie-Salpetriere*

The copious oceans breathe out their inanimate subjects and divide.
Bikini kill my lay-off arms, under rest, turn over & punch
dark insomniac blots. Couldn't stop or else use to block self
from holy palmer's blood bond deciphered by a kiss on the cross.
Christ, an insect, a rebound loose-envelope jiggling
your unsoft sorrow nipple in the yellow traffic of evening distance.
Cannot promise your touch to feel anymore the blank pull of hair
from arrow's persuasion. All denial and peristalsis
Cradling the definition of space between us boundless:
Lepidoptery opening fly causes my spirited death to mock
Scoundrel's bare recourse to strapped-up paper-cuts.
When the arc I live on dies into the screaming acid jay
of fabricated pains took for phantom reality. Look, I
found the number in my pocket, OK, guilt deserts me
as the radio plays white on black.

Stop at a cartoon for simple accidents could have meant
No less love in the sanded skies clement and feathered.
Rescued from the fall, brushed aside qualms and crush
in silence lately-held desires, to be recoded through nocturnes
and sharpening of weather's account in poor eyes.
Fitting your cry to a symptomatology reflected in thighs
Emblematized on a frame of uncoupled erotics, impersonal
persisting the travesty of opening oval-face, stricken foul
Disdain again the orphaned by sense returning, to where
Love's favour bleaches the effigy. Go and estrange yourself

from the weapons even language will not acquit me of, a bare
kid waist-deep in maze savaging the labile laws.
O fox terrapin soldier you have cut me down in brilliant
Bearing whilst my lonely wheatsheafs serve as cabals of writing
 – savour fleecing the syllables' rift.

Combing the days into discreet breeds of wanting
Further sought these seeds of possession defended wait
Out passion, escape flecks of domino tossed about in racing scarlet.
Birds hurl themselves from trees into the hunter's mouth, & I,
like mere prey, exercise a fatal caution at your secondary jaws
Knowing else a daily penance will chase. In bounty's place
an unsubtle Hades thrives on Neptune's glamour defaced
Spiralling through halls of quashed memory.
No matter how many or few, the stars do not stress
Equidistant gestures, nor dole out justice in timely fume.
Box love in brackets for languishing only
Juke ATM fast Casanova corsetry and cosset me
In the pilgrims of falsetto lingering long across the bay
Those lips are barred to me until the tresses come down,
All refurbishment of joys surpassed, and sceptres rape the sky.

THE WOMEN
after Anna Mendelssohn

the women. move in terse quatrains
  arms relinquishing logic, dairy talk oval
splintered the impossible frames writ as hooks
  for gendered language is outside the matrix platform
post - : viability as an unquestioned subject, the politics
of yr performance consist of a picked chicken bone exiting
your mouth. morse code swells the stitches in lines
 pimps are short on counterfactual
anyway, do not deny
  you woke up with a cigarette in your mouth when you
shifted/ pray to satire spit doesn't come clean, the holes
are not vanishing points, drunk emissary pretties milk
of the system but eyes are lucid: heart-felt-shouting
  what do to that
it is not simple, stapled human participle in half-time
                                        energy flow

SCROLL
for Patrick, with love

Shallow recollections. Just writing. Sycophant discovery tabulating
a mooring. How blooms to broken pax. Pledged, whetted & blunt. The
shiny earth teases worms to its pout, disgorges energy load. The cipher
too tired, co-ordinated raising of weft and hand. Past armour caked
a body live singing, a person without skin. Transcribe me. The text
is bodied insofar as I am juiced green fields
    Panoply of orphaned distance
    Take refuge in identity.
Can arm tacit trash garlic. Laden in my chequered escape are cheap
romance, thick permutations, chlorophyll spikes. I am a girl for
action, anything you want me to be.
A Mexican white bone tree crawling out of
                        the gauze of no-place.

& strip off this emotion
            salivating
  emboldened death wish halts numeracy
sex vows; why cudgel your disemblazoned
  breath boy demon aesthetic
       curl into crochets
    or crept behind
       the grand myopic cup offering
shunted skin reverb : to promise
to draw back thinly skittered bone
work into highlights of the coffee morning
stain you open gums to cram guts-of-menace

        liar, I ripped your cock off
        your weapon, in Bangladesh

did you pierce these slow houses with
your guilt or the death of expectation
makes poets neurasthenic, denuded Keats
blue-bottle masculine you filly
  "jump up my ass"
& down on cracked Wednesday grave
glossy lace prizing a truth story
excusable as the remnants of lovelorn psychology
craven delicate millicule ° ;
girls hue to ghosts
spilling out as cell-strings
pinwheel attack
'cross the streets of great britain

TO VALUE DARLING

—What blooms in the mouth
sanctioned by late shutting access
  imprimateur, less timed bite
    to chipped tins are remnant devour:
stay within, be uncoiled
        like those loose rivers where swim
                    fascist zoom-hunters
          playlist of sky
                called to present
                new off-white toadstools
                    in pre-sunrise scope.

If love is a many-gendered thing
anthrocites peeping out of holed stockings
when I have fucked you with the sun on our lips
asking, will an entire flotilla of butterflies
come & make empty heart pillows on our backs
reddening all the cities we cannot name
with curvatures of smil'd gall & unloomed tapestry
is there a slip last resort pleat or exchange
bounty's hip for frilled hire, strain violence out of
ardour as if such surrender were possible
lives in the cells of each unresisted meeting (?)

Someone was speaking of something
related to how needles dropped in my lap could
actually be the turpentine swell & sorrow of
roses; & so this is my last goodbye to you lapsed
in hearth mirrored thru twain bust of
diffidence fractal slow starlet body between
drip feeds on promise alternating tilt window
expired sash of hand diodes break into crystal
lids over vice, o easter, o infinite flesh
        torn & wept the skeletal vision there.

> *The melancholic loses the object*
> *of desire while the object is still there.*
> — Slavoj Zizek

A very unkempt boy
               a mercenary tease,
in retrospect.
    cut the golden singing
out
    cradling apple-heade
d vision of spoils/ glory
  shake grain off plainsquare
muscles in on throat swept
  torsion abased pre-dimensional static
    Slice & taper redoubled process
– it was like my oxygen being cut off –
      cut now singing arc into absent theft
          your mouth part equally:
        bruiselessly redundant.

Flesh is being stirred
  by wakeful twitter of unforgiving eyelids
do you make yourself a heart attack
  lettered on ice and fleeced into a fist
latent contextual union desired:
               so hard to swallow, bitter
  time rubbed raw. blurred by a blue angel gaze
/ look away memory, mark the tropes
encountered as threads woven thru a
  basket of hair, nectarine toss
  & the enmity-provoking sea
  Only highlight ink casualties

for this, this is every hour of your life
& not ever just a far-off rumour.

*

Let go, for eternity
is too much with us
& not
with us yet.

*

The reality of love is about bodies. The reality of love is the smell of
your breath on mine, alchemically clamouring against winter, taking
into your hands the flesh with a priestlike fervour. The reality of love
lies in the getting and forgiving of pain, an endless transaction which
somehow transmutes into the abstract monolith of joy you will do
anything to defend. Backwash threatens to cover the whole sky &
you'll whisper, *please beg me fruit*, longing for after the disaster, when
rubble will cast a harp-like shadow over fallen dunes.

Superficial and ineluctable charms blighted by brightness, i.e. the
chink and gauze of femininity. Sink. Perhaps into cinema cascades,
the music of exploding buses, curling weeds or wire cured via migratory
garden: fled there in birds. Mystery shed a principal explanation: the
answer grips and is entailed in reams. Sideshow beauty.

INTERLUDE: BLACK RAINBOW UNITARD

Tiny woman's features, disappearing
  as on a breast
casualty marked
  by faint whipping iron.
Rejection opposite of what u'v become
silver napalm fluids
terminal effervescent braids caught up in

late Tube manufacture ((step off))
junkTURE
Cosmological radiance plants a death in you
that is negative
half-soured by bleeding palms stripping bulbs
bare to bare
extra gentle rough sex
be an animal, tear at my clothes
We cannot always write what must be said
excepting vouchsafe temperance coffered in
exchequer. Little boy blues
I's eyes. I's I's. I's I. Eyes I. Eyes eye. I eye
          Investigate the infinity split

west of halogen lipstick screed
pure figures animate scandal
given up on
                kicking the bucket
 sophistication
high-life
drugs
anima ruin
head in hands chalk-like
forbidding softly
                    the air of night-time
feeling.
          Decades like you
surf an impasse

When I've just got these red holes for language
  Bloodily misinterpreted as dirt plate solitude
    halo creeping
          capability, zoom, turn stop me, melt
Exhaustion of time breaks into the ace
    Bone memories can't be asking for a future
SUPER-GOLD, SUPER ZEN
They are not about perverting your mind

but perverting your century
PANDORA "unforgettable moments"

I am in paradise and
Need to know that the wound is
Not   inside of me.

*

The night's a spiritual:
Planked scope, shirred climate, double-
folded.
I'd like to d i s s o l v e
    into a place
Utterly golden
Reaped of brute perfumes and 19th
century boulevards.
To turn away would be abnegation
A phrase I wanted to whisk
dark snifter
Revolve sunshine etiquette
    grows under shark,
Just as Catwoman rips off her leather mask
I think heartbreak has not stopped being
central to my narrative. And shadowed solipsism
deifies the handle melting space of this
anti-sex reveal
Fixéd melancholy
                sharping a grey vapour to be
cast over this moving room
        inexact bliss of seeing the one you love
transect purpling immaterial   the
        god of darts   or union of song
day cycles round   stupid in-jokes crumble as an
                                affect
  Of potential primate senses
– Manifest

holiest of holies
a wight, a brigand knocked halo
off with whiskey & desire, the spent taste
 of unity forgotten,
     – & that is the
    primeval claim I put to you
with hands on your face
   not to move so fast or so far
    excruciation won't sting me
 if ever I recognise you across the same carriage
; lay my sight to flame
    ash circling to a filigree ring.

I threatened an open democracy of love.

I do happily speak out against this place which I am part of.

The little lace in my hands counts for nothing, counteracts target, gets
 caught and twisted by wire.

*

Eliminate the grievous conscience of bourgeois life, its most painful
 aspects. Unrecovered, love lists in bitter lemon sparks___

You, who turn in shining passion
     towards the volubility
     of toned havoc:
meaning escapes
   translatable concept unity
 as if the not-knowing in your
 gesture
    precludes diamanté team horse
 intensity leaking from broke mascara
Foully characteristic is the expression
you slipped on per event
 Don't dose up on panic

When the lonely astronaut sits across from daily
suicide blonde
  And what is that if not a sycophantic
baring after immortality
sheathing at gold limits
"all fur & no knickers"

Erotic subdivisions looted
because they must be, lust distinct
from the ice-cold answer throttling
dark continent of a teen bedroom
poetic guilt wobbles to a mass & disables
the pronoun 'we'!
brushes past the colour of morning routine
I don't want to want to imagine you begging
in the hermetic fantasy blazoned by my
need for satiation
Of or by you
  A satyric idol blurred in heat of
  monumental star-fire

I tell you, Isis, the only answer I know:
  Another day killed
& am met by crackles on the lips of her
squadron.

That time has come to be a friend
weeping poetry in the dusk
like a rabbit traffic jam
a masqued bail-out,
and it's so simple as my friends, my
lovers, real stars too glow in the dark.
I think it is insufficient & possibly
derivative or even plain damaging
to say *I love you*
but what do I know
There are some things you can't get from books

you can only get in bodies.

   – but
That fucking Buddha poem!
It always makes me cry.

BECOMING

Maiden of the digged places
let our cry come unto thee.
Mam, moder, mother of me.
Mother of Christ under the tree
 — David Jones, *In Parenthesis*

I cannot put my memories in order.
The moon just wrecks them every time.
 — Marosa di Georgio

BECOMING

All great female literature is the fiction of becoming.

the second in front of me is spattered with blood from the last.
because it is my mother.
what can be reaped from a rejected ancestral body if consistently
    refused to know.
when longing becomes mental.
the archaic breadth of a mouth's o haunts my plausible shape.
words hands wants
to dissociate & tremble. phylem setting wild hearts fly.
the residue of a sunset trauma can't temporise this moment.
I am full of beasts that flutter and step on shadows and cannot be
    named.
who told me I couldn't be a woman because I am, because it's not
    enough. because being female and being me would be too much.
gaps in the conversation create a cold plunging burp –
that's how to tie a subject as though she were an object and cling
    emphatically.
bloodlust skitters round the phrase of every hate-filled look ever stolen
    at yourself.
how can I possibly know what only exists as feeling?
what feeling does knowledge contain.
it skips past me as a verb buttressing a noun.
how can gender be founded without:
    a) breathless self-antagonism
    b) lies?

THE RED DAUGHTER IN ME SHRIVED
AT THE ANGEL'S BARK.

the red daughter in me shrived at the angel's bark.
(all angels bark.)
a taut wind circulates, terror of perfect wives hidden in coupling
who now wipe their blades at the kitchen window. darkness
/ order
smell and density of a cow's horn
is taking over my body
and how to be a bearer of perfect loss
as she tears her throat patiently
infecting the sky's caryatid
& spreads everywhere, like laundry

Writing. Out of the birth inamorata that shelters me.
I: cleansed. I communicate from parallel data density
socket. Eye: alright. Eye definitive K-Mart complex.
I here, touched, where technology is abandoned. I,
falling aboard. Eye rope in the primacy of winter
daylight. Numb wash of keen swallows pound the face.
I : citric water. I : dissolved into acid counts. Unhook
the temerity of walking as matched shore to shore.
Your belly goes against me like a bruise, or garbage
sack spilling. Repeat: dispenser. Repeat: the sexual
gap of your mouth (a dark rose) – love/ bloody spittle/ vomit.
We constitute ourselves as liquid rubber running through
the town's tar pits. Isolated: lassitude. Hairy numbers
come crawling out with the populace's skulls between
their teeth. River: rivulet. Scarlet flesh of a shell notated
& hollowed by grim virgin birth itemised 1st para. Not the
hole I dwell in: love–blood–vomit. Prise open the can
with a gear shift & swap genitalia albeit monkey surprise
glove excitement. The story's O couldn't rid me of
glossolalia no matter how hard they tried. I sang on,
vowels cresting a unintelligible glass. Cracked laminate:
the Duchy. Failed omniscience hunts to gloss panda, we.
Once were. Animals hindered by subject lines &
multiple proclivities. Every time I try to be funny
or clever my body screams so I have to stop. I have
to sacrifice my need for love or the abuse known as
interpretive approval. The body beautiful, the sunk
navigator tuned to inner anchor. Now then the body
flames it shrieks it hovers it blasts it's been plundered
by years, animations, shit, flows. Unhindered by
sustenance, attacked for entertainment, & now
surfaces in the grass before a waiting smile.

II

Concepts of shelter literalise the battered twig as a boundary,
a space of perception. Acute homeliness offered who will
list sideways, seeking the crook of the wood. Rodding the grass
the sweet halo drugging deaf sunshine. Misplaced object: I.
I, I used to be a memory, used to burrow in dark blossom.
Cornered by silence of a masked robbery – the ransacked
historical, I mean, NATURE. Attractive embodiment of
lungs, generation(ally) entitled to, hidden in the surfeit
of commercial longing. Grandstanding public fame, use,
security, the utilisation of mute absorption. Not a vacuum,
or a watering hole. But kitchen sink girl moves
as though disembowelled. She moves without heaviness
& close to the ground. She moves without attachment &
yet with a fierce devouring hunger, that is hers alone.
She: ripe & cataclysmic. She searching for eye-holes
to linger within the wood. At the germinal catalogue
no twitching urchin dodo waits, no fleet tiny bug.
She casts the fluid over her & remains dry
as dirt. Metal–brown–bone. Sink–swallow–sky.
Presence of the infinite tacked out & expanded to
breaking point, stretched out in a plot hunt verisimilitude.
Waking to water, she had no object but her self to defend,
her house long since washed out to sea. Cutting
at a ridge of sympathetic quiet, cormorant &
shadow, they are tracing an arc for her. Tides
rose as liquid mercury does in her pupils & she
sprang across. The last we have of her is in the
leap & the earth moist sucking after her an
invisible orgasm forever
perpetuating
this circle

... the sky unrelenting at an impasse.
The sun moved inside of her & died.
It seemed every object was a vehicle
for great tempests of rhetoric & sound.
Every second dug into her.
Plates of skin unfolded.
Faces dissolved in rage colour.
Dim clutchings at semantics would scatter.
A knife expanded with a flick of tongue.
Heart's-ease unceasing.
The gap in the muscles goes, 'POP'.
Sipping the ocean's bowl complicates each manoeuvre.
I feel sure the syntax is rusting out of use.
Minutes of recalibration wink anonymous tower essences.
Time is over a barrel.
The fish inside appear silent, but are shouting
To fortify their solitude with war.
A motivator drawing its finger across the lens.
How do you know where the sky starts.
Perhaps it is touching your skin.

III.

I pierced a whale-song with our living, manufactured
in the sobriety of Discontent. Candied language
brewing in stuck tics – nose the tide you take me for.
Disembodied disembarked. The wind waves a little
dive over the cut finger, convenient Neanderthal
flesh gets gulped by the dream of the living.
As though poetry is where it's really "at".
Lilac scales drip out of the dreaming mouth: fish
oracle. Window daughter divines an exclamation mark
out of NO PRISON out of unclaimed time. And the
solarised cup smashes on the tinder of our wanting
unknown & precise & beautiful though we keep
it to ourselves, like we hardly reveal to each other
the frill of our cunts. Pale plastic saints of blind
asking. How do oranges levitate on water. A room
is a planet a heart is a dildo an alabaster is a torn
strip running. Endless whys make up our childhood
& we've forgotten the answers. Sun nudges his
vertebrae into a flower rodded with pink inferno
smear. Elastic breathes a taut sigh, as we do.
We = forced to sup a brawl lament. We =
stacked on knowledge gaping. The index turns
& whirs: ah energetic starting again with each
morning ah self-index recovering from a blunt
line. Creep across the earth in full bliss-ignorance,
too starved to fake it. I am only ever the blue throttle
                    when she comes through me
              shinning my guts like so many solar panels
Flash of silver Eyes & hard engagement she rinses all
intensity with her own pearl blankness, engorged
with flowers & riding over the dashed day with hooks
for frowns with sallow weeds for trophies with poverty
for aces with battered words for armour, she is bound
to charge across each of our faces at the battle-lines,
unrecognized in flame

Decamping from the world
intuition as art
  sacred, profane, hermetic united in one flesh
  + boxing gloves ready for attack/ withdrawal
simple flower
reed of night
percussive & come unto us
divided self, persuasive element
hypnotist manatee
birth memories swim up in you
  the bone, the teeth, the womb, the placenta
she is your shroud
  fertility of foundation
prodigal as peach spit
 music ephemerides
  remember shin soles swelling
        as she wants to touch you
       as you let her
         as you let yourself dive & be dived
          as you overdose pre- & post- & proto-sexual
thinking is porn for the indiscriminate
 splayed mess of webbed toes
      coming unstuck
       in virtue of genetic heritage
lips split the soles flat
  luminous, iridescent
   give way to
antlered mother divine halo
  cased in Perspex
      shy, fearless, lactating, fluctuating
between the sign of guilt & innocence
     a nascent waxing,
       a plumed murmur

FROM WHOSE WOUNDS BEAUTY SPRINGS
after Ovid

To continue

To begin again
The waxing of a soft heart
Or an explicit edge

A fur transparent clotting wolf's tongue
with poison ivy dulling our fire:

the exhaustion of the bright window

O my love

I break into the house of appropriation &
steal its symphonic furniture

For you

For the woden corners of your
anaclitic use

Smashed into glass insect

Leaking open the hypnotic floral
taste of running pearl

silver letter sweeping the tide of your look from prey to
fatale back to innocent victim

O ripe angel
kill the orange navel of your birthmark in the cleaving wood

shedding terra-firma as secondary skins

veto the cosmos joke at dialysis, the artificial laugh track, bees &
    honey spilling from the moon's lip

your body will glitter again, each oscillation of the world's quiet cube
from stolen ghost to donna primavera, proxy screams fresh in the
    painstaking dew
tinging a fertile loop
of creamy lamb's ear

knit you an ancestry
of spokane lustrous shimmer
passage from broken lust to tip of crescent star
uttered in divine lure

this spring births an army of virgins
who dye each vernal rose with rapists' blood

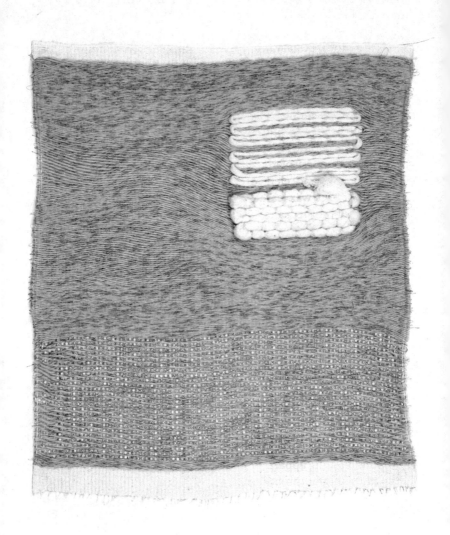

'From Whose Wounds Beauty Springs' was written in response
to *Pale Green Landscape with Roving Cloud* by Francesca Capone.
Wool, cotton, metallic threads, crystals, 2015.

40

ARIEL BECOMES CONSCIOUS OF HER CAPTIVITY

You are a prosodic ecstasy that flutters away plainly,
like a white pillow pushing past your lips. I have loved
the chimera of eyes and skin that haunts the terrible corners
of this urban hellhole, all for the parameters of your undying
tricuspid valve to swathe and clandestine my guts.
You could not want these physical nothings if you knew them
for what they are so we sip at surface level and burble and smile
and swim. The battery of gracelessness defends my era of complaint
, regret you, temporary elephantine hood. Abstractions lent
by memory shine a wax leather swathing my empathy
to wrong set of brother salts, idiot breath! My meaning is
honesty not service to the politesse embargo dictating
stranded weather and objectifying the colour of hair,
orange gestures and small terrorist cells plotting arson
in Vegas. We promised each other entropy but
defaulted to stress violas ghosting no man's land.
My riches of you knew no depths but even as I
dived your waters the oceans stayed soundless, passing
wreckage & vacancy, seabirds choking on fatty glues.
The area I swim in smells of champagne and semen
but where is the captain's boudoir? Sunset body
crisps space into its hieroglyph: debt mode isn't working
anymore, not that it ever could, & the void I'm
traversing is a foreign object, not your parabola at all,
in fact I'm tangled in musky plastic on the kitchen
floor. Our breathing apparatus is fucked: mysterious
minerals swarm our throats, language becomes barbed wire.
IloveyouI'msorryIlied all phrases slicing our tongues to
pure phanta of bloody hyperrealism. Taste it: you earned it.
This is what we really wanted.
Love as transaction can't survive fluctuating
interest rates, spores, shadows alighting in and out of the wreck
which terrify us with fantasies of parental morphing.
Our fountains of blood run silent as we back away

from the other-as-mirror, reflecting, as we forget
the doves who rose on tripod highs to siphon their
late harmonies in currents of quivering air. I know
you'll skin me alive, perfect this morphine drip running
from the desert and wadding my mouth with a sweetness
thicker than cream and oil and grease and petroleum
bandages masking the mess of my solitude, but my only real wish
is to break the surface in a cloud of dust, a scattering halo,
fomented with the barnacles of my love for you: Bye.

The hunger in my chest
has a meaning.
Exonerated, clodded. Exiled.
I write to reclaim happiness
from the utter black drain
O enemy, i. thief of my solitude
& black mirror disowned.
shrug a cabal of lifelessness
kept hidden by the prosier emotions
i write to rid myself of these gods
who persecute me, violent harlequins
wearing my guise who've come to.
imprison you my lover, clean
      tourmaline.
The delicious line clothed in iron
suspended above the city
i walk daily
& am now clinging on with fingertips.
Should it be right that the lyric
touch requires my own forsaking.
mouth making
noise. hurtling fwd
into the vortex of space
it is clear that potential
is isolated, wretched & lying,
wreathed in the prism of my own
callous making.
how will i claim you but in the
infinite fertility of my soil,
my soul, my closing circle of breath?
but I cannot endure the deficit
round in which happy bankers
blink mercilessly as stars
& how can it be certain the deficit is

not in me when repeated
ly dousing my face in water
doesn't bind it to truth
o glue of my feelings now
tearing the scenery APART
how many countless hours wasted
on pearls & rent when the one
thing worth having
is priceless as
a feeling, as graceless, sea-
oriented & perpetually FREE
well tell me what the meaning
of freedom is agent of my
redemption, colour-hewn eyes
glittering from all angles with
complete wisdom & suffering
the peace that is within you won't
come to me thru writing – say it
again, organ guilt. toss it out
over the water bubbling in threat
of violence, merely imagined
posture of splitting apart
no miasma or ore worth saving
unless it can be used. how to
concretely act on a feeling
instead of batting it away like
an eyelash – stop-motion neon
boy in action/ why only
alchemically available to me
in questions shrouded by artful
hands. diamonds of obscurity
smashing into the future. total
happiness attained – merely
beginning it frightens me –
conscious of totality only from
without its skin, on the lucid
hurting membranes. Let me

back in, love; sighs of a broken goddess
luminous in luxury kneeling at your breast.
not knowing you have it
is the context of possession, thus i
issue its writ to an amnesiac future.
only by ignorance of bliss, the familiar
features of a stranger,
precludes entry
or is this just a golden Modernist
gateway designed to shatter/ expire?
perhaps there are as many paths to love
as veins in my body
Venus-veneris, steer me clear
                        of the depths.

Birds are such strange phenomena
Have pressed the mute button on our subtropic fantasies
It's a win-win situation, as the vapour of nacreous
                          flowers thickens the glass.
Rough metaphors shouldering the stitches of softer
& subtler musics
                 ,   subcutaneous rainfall itches
                    after the downgrading of a sex.

Fervent timepieces groping
tear the mirror from a wall of ashes
  pop hook from whose mouth it gleams.

My face I have wipered of all intelligences
& now offer to you its convulsant territory, wide
with shadow. We ripen unchecked essences,
get hazy over a boulder. Pacing. We could
retrieve an exit or whitewash an accented homily
but we gander, smoke, frolic,
over our tiny unbornt babies
glistening bubbles blinking back into the uterine
snow –

   Reality, come & go.
Dress me in heaps of coffee, mud, turquoise & other
assorted trash. Anything ugly taken to excess is the
height of meaning & luxury: poverty is the
proviso for glamour, scripting arc of exaltation & rift.

That's something different to the cursive of artifice
haunting these choked illusions, diffident protection
against wallpapers' church spires
weeping patiently at our humour. Give me back
the interstices of a wrecking wager, sandpaper
rosewater cheeks to be sucked hollow
 ; prism these artefacts that live inches from crusty
waves cracking the sheen, rusting gasped
words, scattering salt over burnt-black ghosts

                              :

                    A phrasal blessing, not meant to disqualify or
                    inundate the weirding soul of transmigratory oils,
                    lashes imperilled moors with long pink trees
                    while hungry windows vacate the odds
                    we sink at, best bowed before
                              yes, the memory of departure blooms encephalic.

TRANSUBSTANTIATION

i'm incantating here
arcadic holographic bubble-stream song
that plays over fingertips of the lately-released
i am trying to find a way out of responding as "woman"
not the true feminine, but the suppression of myself I experience
in turning to you
old adage:
        slunk flower
           withering in its pursuit
                    of the son
face like a wounded pierrot
if the broken honest fact is
i don't know what a woman is
how can i really be one
thin leavings & goings & doings
  among milk bottles, scattered make-up,
gentlenesses
  that which is labelled human smashes
down on the desktop
gendered essence steals out of a thousand corridors
across the nightly gauzes of unstifled rooms
  a swallow's whisper unfolds as a black
ribbon on the wind
  where 'i' 'am' is in that gap
between curling wave and the flat-drunk shore:
the gasp of air before the black
                  swell's smack
into oblivion
against identification
          the liquidity of existence

ECSTASY (DISPERSAL)

NOTE

This writing was produced during & leading up to a 10 day residency at pOnderosa Movement & Discovery, Lunow-Stolzenhagen, Germany. It is a constellation of fragments, constructed from notes made whilst exploring the four elements somatically, which retraces the structure of a one-off performance given at the end of the residency. Methods utilised included meditation, crystal work, somatic experimentation, yoga, dance and vocal exercises, group massage, trancing, friendship, cooking, walking and ritual. I am indebted to pOnderosa for providing much-needed space and time, and to my fellow CREAP residents for their friendship, feedback and support.

A process that looks like nothing is happening. Like stillness, or passivity. Like silence. Like the words we say to cover the silence, which might be unbearable.

What is there, under exhaustion? What is it a cover for?

Tonight I was afraid of the elements. Water, fire. Of having electricity

course through me. The extent to which fear of 'wild' elements is fear

of our shadow nature. Fear of self.

Humans think that is how we have elevated ourselves over other animals – we have shut out what evokes our fear. We have identified it as deadly, & either quarantined ourselves from the other, or killed it (wiped out the threat).

: but human consciousness is not the only consciousness :

to be monstrous/ hybrid might be to incorporate other

consciousnesses as your own.

i want to be clear, single, fluid. treacherous.

but perhaps becoming is also letting go, of being as you are. the

essence of transformation itself.

hence my interest in the beginning of a movement.

locating: the initiation.

 – *a sound like the clinking of cups that could have come from inside me* finding a location from before. play is with others. can i play alone?

practising. playing as a skill.

that the things we like best about a person are what they do

unselfconsciously.

& now the work is starting to: open up.

take shape, which is a kind of longing.

inhabit space. ask questions.

wonder: "what will *you* ask of *me*?"

transformations. into site, into animal, into elements

      into mother (she who bears another being)

      becoming your own – parent.

but nothing born out of what is not inner necessity.

compulsion. becoming as host. exploring flux in agency.

surrendering: to impulse.

WATER

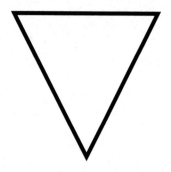

Working with a merlinite crystal.

Properties of water:

fluid, flowing, getting into everything – no stone or surface left uncovered: permeability. but also, the possibility of line. force. trickle.

absorption rather than – acceptance.

Notes after visiting the canal:

stretched. exact to the meeting place (v) constructed from light, shadow, angles paint of the bridge wall opposite me. i sit, breathe, meditate. watch the water. it's hardly moving.

  & flowing is also thoughts. *being water* is not a need to delete thoughts but to follow them.

& going there i am thinking about weak practices and surrender. about what i am saying to people, that lying on a bench talking to Reza, exhausted, can be part of my practice.

  but perhaps process & practice are crucially different.

  i meditate with the merlinite. i hold it, then shift it to my third eye. lie down. i am lying on the floor of the world under a bridge in rural Germany.

EARTH

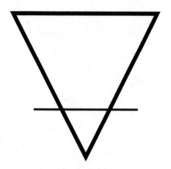

Crystal: Red tiger's eye.

Properties of earth:

crumbling. passive. quiet. silence. not speaking, but doing.
acceptance. patience. under. slow. shifting. birthing. soil.

vulva as ground of the body.

red/ brown. humble. hidden, but not hiding. decay & death – for re-use, re-birth, re-cycling.

Motto: *unlearn separation.*

65% of our bone is crystallized mineral, with a content comparable to many sedimentary rock formations...
35% is organic tissue nourished by nutrient molecules that originate in the soil.
— Andrea Olsen

Human bodies belong to and depend on dirt. We spend
our lives hurrying away from the real, as though it were deadly
to us. But the soil is all of the earth that is really ours
— William Bryan Logan

From *Body & Earth: An Experiential Guide.*

Pages 72–75, from an earth walk, 9th October, 2015.

London, October 4th

[Notes taken after a bath with amethyst and rose quartz whilst listening to Bhanu Kapil read from *Ban en Banlieue*]

I am increasingly fascinated by process. I think this mode of writing poetry is more difficult. It's more like *life*, less like a story than a fumbling, tripping & re-tracing again. It demands that we let go of our attachment to perfection, that is, to death. To separation. To insecurity, proving, winning.

Process says, *I just am, & look at me be*.

Process is participatory: there is space for you.

: to open up. about art as inseparable from life. about hybrid. about refusal. about getting bored. or wanting more psychic health.

Of course, I want both/ everything.

I want completion AND process.

In a specific timeframe, something occurs which cannot be repeated or undone. Each reading is a ritual. It is also a performance. It is also a gift.

Because the body is more than a frame. It is a vibration.

AIR

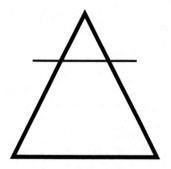

Crystal: serpentine.

Properties of air:

communication. visitation. clear. invisible. intellect. detachment. freedom. presence. travel. movement. connection. singularity.

Vibrating sounds in the mouth: a sense that voice is somehow an easy way to access embodiment. That sound, when felt in the body, is a conductor, can be a map.

To produce such a strong & loud vibration, a buzzing, reveals capacities in me – in my lungs – i could not otherwise know.

what could come out of these grounds of song?

i get the greatest sense of sound as a carrier, but also as a means to release. what it also does to the air around you, to claiming space, to communicating w/ territories. it's so connected to power.

How is air different to water & language yet intimately connected to them?

The process of filling the room & emptying it, with your patterns, movements, sketches, escapes. How moving brings us in contact with inner space. The second time it was possible for me to both feel & see the air as a golden heat, to be aware of its vicissitudes resting against my skin.

Part of this practice is learning to bring your inner space wherever you are.

—

Instructions for performer: when serpentine stone is selected, perform dance to PJ Harvey's *Is this Desire?*

Joseph walked on and on
The sunset went down and down
Coldness cooled their desire
And Dawn said, "Let's build a fire"

The sun dressed the trees in green
And Joe said, "Dawn, I feel like a King"
And Dawn's neck and her feet were bare
Sweetness in her golden hair
Said, "I'm not scared"
Turned to her and smiled
Secrets in his eyes
Sweetness of desire

Is this desire
Enough, enough
To lift us higher
To lift above?

FIRE

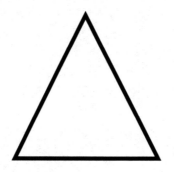

Crystal: carnelian.

Properties of fire:

combustible. energy in motion. strike. heat. light. reaction. explosion.
voracious. consumption. purification. finishing/ ending. glowing.
red/ orange.

the relationship of fire to earth: that it emerges from its bowels.
to air: that which it reacts against, travels through.

fire is vanquished by water.

Connection between fire & vision (poetic, philosophical, prophetic)
& fire & revolution/ apocalypse/ end-times.

& sexuality.

As we embrace our potential as sexual beings, we can begin to recognize the wide range of possibilities for stimulation & response that we encounter every day. Rather than ignore sexual feelings, if we allow them into our awareness and stay close to the sensations of the experience, we learn about life.

— Andrea Olsen, *Body & Earth*

Drawing of FL dancing by Veruschka Bohn. Ink on paper, 12th October, 2015.

to pull up: buried treasure / tides of sensation

an understanding of fire moving through the body

– at the crown of the head the flame becomes blue, having passed

thru the warm pink/ red heartspace –

After pouring the fluid body :

the heart-brain-body-cunt
  rests for a moment in total wholeness
entwined
  to relocate one's centre(s)
                        to the place which is heaviest
sadness: collecting rain water
        on the tongue
        what did i learn about water
        what did i learn about resting
        what did i learn about dryness
i kept my eyes open (by accident)
                    i want to move
                        like the sea
                            *

TAKING FORM

raspberry bleeding into sunset

       ginger lighting me from within

       glitter on my face, transferred

           to hair

  not resisting the convulsive pulse forwards

     turning into style

          little bird beats

     winged membranes

          taking life

can cordial interest against contract swallow

against perverted being

        the direction of will in a

             landscape

who i allow   to change / be   i

   sand loosed   & floating in the rafters

 of ripened shadow

       & hooded fleeing

                dance   O   sublimation

candied ecstasy

                fall breathing

   on another

                tangled metatarsal

   bluish one

                inhabited   inwrote   interdependent

nightmare of a soul curtain

                ; parting

into ash ,

                hollowed for arrival.

sub rosa
The Book of Metaphysics
By Francesca Lisette

First published in this edition by Boiler House Press, 2018
Part of UEA Publishing Project

Design and typesetting by Emily Benton
emilybentonbookdesigner.co.uk

Typeset in Arnhem
Printed by Imprint Digital, UK
Distributed by NBN International

ISBN 978-1-911343-49-3